PUBLIC LIBRARY DISTRICT OF COLUMBIA

W9-BUX-646

Let's Look at Prairie Dogs

Christine Zuchora-Walske

Lerner Publications Company
Minneapolis

Copyright © 2010 by Lerner Publishing Group, Inc.

All rights reserved. International copyright secured. No part of this book may be reproduced, stored in a retrieval system, or transmitted in any form or by any means — electronic, mechanical, photocopying, recording, or otherwise — without the prior written permission of Lerner Publishing Group, Inc., except for the inclusion of brief quotations in an acknowledged review.

Lerner Publications Company
A division of Lerner Publishing Group, Inc.
241 First Avenue North
Minneapolis, MN 55401 U.S.A.

Website address: www.lernerbooks.com

Library of Congress Cataloging-in-Publication Data

Zuchora-Walske, Christine.
    Let's look at prairie dogs / by Christine Zuchora-Walske.
        p.   cm. — (Lightning bolt books™ – Animal close-ups)
    Includes index.
    ISBN 978-0-7613-3891-8 (lib. bdg. : alk. paper)
        1. Prairie dogs—Juvenile literature. I. Title.
    QL737.R68Z836 2010
    599.36'7—dc22   2008051856

Manufactured in the United States of America
1 2 3 4 5 6 — BP — 15 14 13 12 11 10

Contents

Not Really a Dog

Look! An animal is peeking out of a hole in the ground. Can you guess what kind of animal it is?

This animal is a prairie dog.
It is not really a dog. It is
more like a squirrel.

This prairie dog lives in South Dakota.

A prairie dog has a fat, furry body and a short tail.

Prairie dog fur is golden brown.

Prairie dogs eat grass and other plants.

They pick and eat the plants with their sharp claws and teeth.

Prairie dogs have strong claws on each foot.

Tunnel Diggers

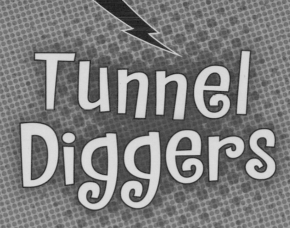

Prairie dogs also use their claws and teeth to dig burrows. Burrows are underground tunnels. Prairie dogs live in burrows.

A prairie dog sleeps in its burrow.

As a prairie dog digs, it throws dirt out of its burrow.

What will it do with all this dirt?

The prairie dog makes a round
hill of dirt called a mound.
The mound makes a ring
around the burrow hole.

This prairie dog
has finished
digging its burrow.

A place with many mounds is called a prairie dog town.

The mound helps keep rain from flooding the burrow. What else is a mound good for?

A prairie dog can sit on a mound and watch for predators. Predators are animals that hunt and eat other animals.

Three prairie dogs keep careful watch for predators.

Being Hunted

A badger is sneaking near. Badgers eat prairie dogs.

Like prairie dogs, badgers dig. A badger will dig to catch a prairie dog.

CHIRK! A prairie dog barks when it sees a predator. Other prairie dogs listen and look around.

If a predator comes too near, prairie dogs rush underground. They wait and listen.

This prairie dog is hiding in a burrow.

The prairie dogs hear the predator go away.

They peek to make sure the predator is gone.

17

YIP! It is safe to come out now!

18

When prairie dogs bark messages about predators, they help their families stay safe.

One prairie dog always keeps watch for predators while other prairie dogs eat.

Prairie Dog Families

A prairie dog family is called a coterie. A coterie lives together in one or more burrows.

These prairie dogs belong to the same coterie.

Prairie dogs in a coterie do many things to stay close.
They kiss.

A prairie dog mother and baby kiss by touching noses.

They groom one another to keep their fur clean and neat.

Prairie dogs groom by licking and touching one another's fur.

They play together. They rest together too. **How does your family stay close?**

young prairie dogs play on their mound.

Baby Prairie Dogs

Baby prairie dogs called pups are born underground in the spring. Six weeks later, they come outside for the first time.

Prairie dog pups stay safe in a burrow.

Pups stay near their mother. She teaches them how to find food and stay safe as they grow.

Prairie dog pups cuddle up to their mother.

Pups nurse as they grow. Nursing is drinking milk from the mother's body.

This prairie dog pup is nursing.

By fall, the pups are grown up. They can dig, bark, and peek. They can help their coterie in many ways.

Young prairie dogs learn to find their own food.

27

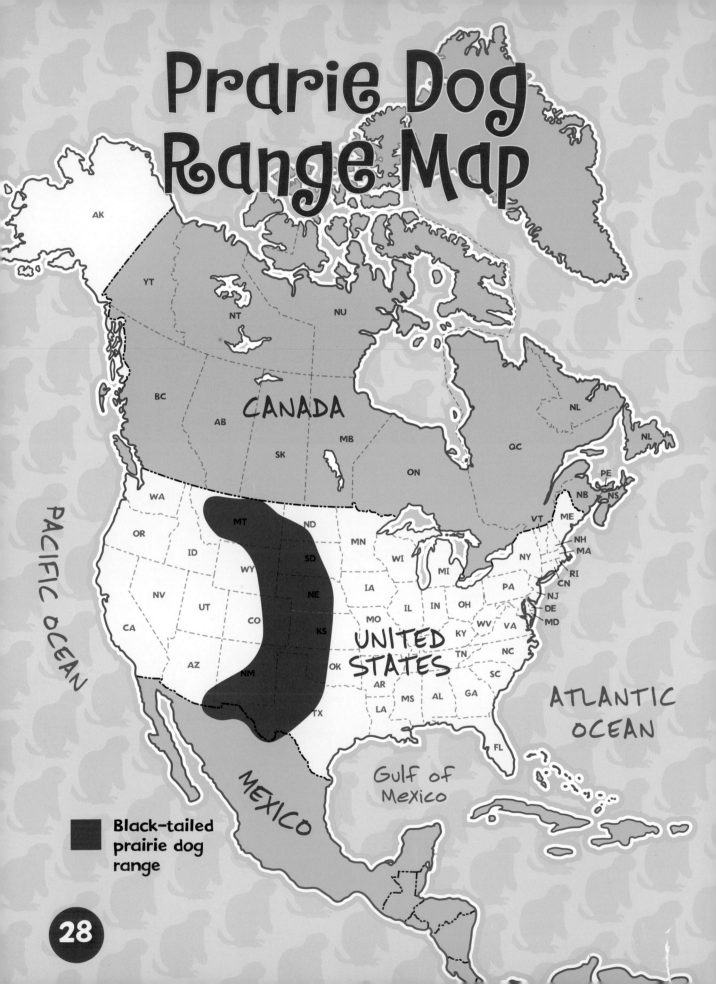

Prarie Dog Range Map

AK

YT

NT

NU

BC

AB

CANADA

SK

MB

ON

QC

NL

NL

PE

NB

NS

WA

MT

ND

VT

ME

OR

ID

MN

NH

MA

WY

SD

WI

MI

NY

RI

NV

UT

NE

IA

PA

CN

CO

IL

IN

OH

NJ

CA

KS

MO

WV

VA

DE

MD

AZ

NM

OK

UNITED STATES

KY

TN

NC

TX

AR

SC

MS

AL

GA

LA

PACIFIC OCEAN

ATLANTIC OCEAN

FL

MEXICO

Gulf of Mexico

Black-tailed prairie dog range

Prairie Dog Diagram

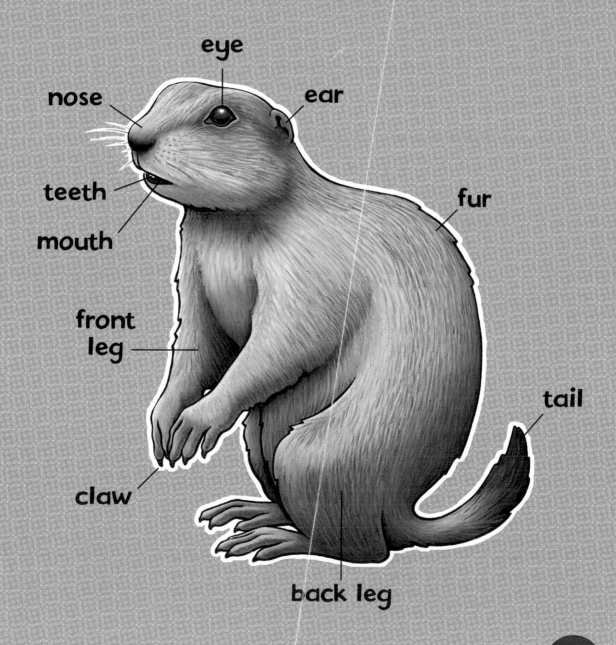

eye

nose

ear

teeth

mouth

fur

front leg

tail

claw

back leg

Glossary

burrow: an underground tunnel where some animals live

coterie: a prairie dog family

groom: to keep fur clean and neat

mound: a round hill of dirt that makes a ring around a prairie dog burrow

nurse: to drink mother's milk

predator: an animal that hunts and eats other animals

pup: a baby prairie dog

Further Reading:

Doudna, Kelly. *It's a Baby Prairie Dog!* Edina, MN: Abdo, 2008.

Enchanted Learning: Prairie Dog
http://www.enchantedlearning.com/subjects/
mammals/rodent/Prairiedogprintout.shtml

Gaarder-Juntti, Oona. *What Lives in the Prairie?*
Edina, MN: Abdo, 2009.

McGehee, Claudia. *A Tallgrass Prairie Alphabet.*
Iowa City: University of Iowa Press, 2004.

National Geographic: Prairie Dog
http://animals.nationalgeographic.com/animals/
mammals/prairie-dog.html

San Diego Zoo's Animal Bytes: Prairie Dog
http://www.sandiegozoo.org/animalbytes/
t-prairie_dog.html

Index

Photo Acknowledgments

The images in this book are used with the permission of: © Norma Cornes/Dreamstime.com, p. 1; © Henk Bentlage/Dreamstime.com, pp. 2, 25; © Erik Snyder/Photonica/Getty Images, p. 4; © Bates Littlehales/National Geographic/Getty Images, p. 5; © Sergio Pitamitz/Robert Harding World Imagery/Getty Images, p. 6; © Alan Briere/SuperStock, p. 7; © age fotostock/SuperStock, pp. 8, 20; © Dr. John Cunningham/Visuals Unlimited, Inc., p. 9; © Frank Greenaway/Dorling Kindersley/Getty Images, p. 10; © Larry West/FLPA, p. 11; © John & Barbara Gerlach/Visuals Unlimited, Inc., p. 12; © John Foxx/Stockbyte/Getty Images, p. 13; © Tom Brakefield/SuperStock, p. 14; © G. Richard Kettlewell/America 24-7/Getty Images, p. 15; © Rui Matos/Dreamstime.com, p. 16; © Mark Newman/SuperStock, p. 17; © John Cornell/Visuals Unlimited, Inc., p. 18; © Marta Johnson, p. 19; © Beth Davidow/Visuals Unlimited, Inc., p. 21; © Raymond K. Gehman/National Geographic/Getty Images, pp. 22, 23; © W. Perry Conway/CORBIS, p. 24; © Russell Graves, p. 26; © Jeff Foott/Discovery Channel Images/Getty Images, p. 27; © Laura Westlund/Independent Picture Service, pp. 28, 29; © Dave Massey/Dreamstime.com, p. 30; © Holly Kuchera/Dreamstime.com, p. 31.

Front cover: © M. & C. Photography/Peter Arnold, Inc. (main). © Bates Littlehales/National Geographic/Getty images (background).

JUN 10 REC'D